THE DREAMING I

AN INTERACTIVE DREAM JOURNAL

BY KEZIA VIDA

D1528031

Want more information about how you can develop a transformative dream practice and get more out of this book?

Visit KeziaVida.com/thedreamingi. There you'll find a free introductory video about how to use this journal, a free mini course about How to Remember Dreams, and information about The Dreaming I Workshop, a 28-day journey with this journal to cultivate a powerful relationship with your dreams.

Scan the code above to learn more!

THE

PRACTICE OF

DREAMING

If there is one thing I love most about dreams, it is how personal and specific they are to each individual. Gather a room of 20 people, and you will easily have 20 different perspectives on what dreams are and what they mean.

The deeply internal and intimate nature of dreams can make them challenging to teach and write about. At the start of most classes or workshops I hold, I feel compelled to remind people that whatever I offer, if it doesn't resonate with their own dreaming experience, then they should feel free to ignore it completely. My central appraoch to dreams is to surrender to them fully and allow them to work in the particular way they desire to--knowing that one way may not ever look like someone else's.

All that said, I have developed four principles that I operate by when doing dream work. These principles are the backbone of this journal. I believe and trust in these principles for pragmatic reasons: I have seen that when I abide by them, they make growth, healing, and transformation possible. That is why I wish to share them, and why I created this journal--to support you in developing a relationship with your dreams that has depth, power, and nourishes the deepest parts of who you are.

PRINCIPLE 1: NO ONE WILL EVER UNDERSTAND A DREAM BETTER THAN THE DREAMER. No one has the dream you had precisely the way you had it. Your dream experience is wholly yours, and, crucially, of you. Everything that is observed or felt in the dream is, by definition, an aspect of your consciousness.

PRINCIPLE 2: DREAMS SHINE LIGHT ON THE ASPECTS OF OUR SELVES THAT WE RESIST, DENY, OR AVOID. If we are feeling stuck in certain areas of our lives, we may have difficulty seeing our dream from a clear perspective. Knowing that the dream may be revealing something we're trying to avoid is a great step to breaking it open.

PRINCIPLE 3: ALL DREAMS ARE CREATED EQUAL AND SHOULD BE TREATED AS SUCH. I have found it is vital to my own dreamwork that I do not judge one dream as better than any other. The risk is too great when we begin to rank our dreams, we risk missing out on the hidden depths contained in the ones we throw away.

PRINCIPLE 4: ALL DREAMS ARISE WITH AN INTENTION TO HEAL, TRANSFORM, INSPIRE, AND/OR PRECIPITATE GROWTH. When I trust that dreams have this potential, I have seen life-changing results–for myself and so many others. So, I continue to trust, and dreams continue to reveal the powerful medicine, vision, and strength that they offer.

USE THIS BOOK

ABOUT THE DREAMING I

This book is a hybrid of a journal and a workbook. My deepest hope is that you'll find your way to integrate the exercises and offerings into your life, bringing color to these pages as you go on a deep and intimate journey with your dreams. There are three types of pages in the journal: Daily Dream Feel pages, Specific Dream pages, and Open Dream pages.

OPEN DREAM PAGES (PG. 10) Starting on page 11 of this book you'll find blank pages for you to record your dreams however you would like. If you are busy in the morning, jotting down 2-3 nouns when you first wake up can help ensure that you'll be able to remember the dream later when you have more time to record it.

DAILY DREAM PAGES (PG. 95) You will find these pages marked as explore starting on page 95. They are my favorite format to improve your dream recall and begin to integrate your dreams into your life. They ask you to look at your dream from two perspectives--from an objective point of view, and a subjective point of view. From your senses, and from your heart.

SPECIFIC DREAM PAGES (PG. 180) There are 10 different exercise pages that were created for you to explore depending on the type of dream experience you recently had. Refer to the table on page 181 when you want to dive deeper with a particular dream. You can also take the instructions on these pages and complete on separate papers or other journals.

ABOUT THE AUTHOR

Kezia Vida began training in the Natural Dreamwork tradition in 2009. In 2013, she began shamanic and ceremonial work, completing the year long training program with the Power Path in 2018. Her understanding of dreams is a blend of Jungian influences and shamanic, indigenous perspectives. She splits her time between her home in New Orleans and 111 acres in rural Mississippi outside the city. There, she works with her husband to offer retreats and workshops about dreamwork, connecting with nature, and righting our relationship with mother earth and the resources that sustain our lives. She believes that through deeper connection with our dreams, we can more easily connect to our truth, and in doing so manifest the changes necessary for a more life-nourishing future for our planet.

INTRO

Learn more about her work:

www.KeziaVida.com

 &   @KeziaVida

OPEN DREAM PAGES

RECORD To start your dream practice, begin by writing your dreams down. A lot of dreamers do not have time in the morning to record dreams. Start by jotting down three nouns -- a person in the dream, a place where you were, or a thing that you witnessed or interacted with in your dream time. Record them when you first wake up in the space provided. Then you can come back and write the whole dream down later in the day when you have more time.

Dreamers developing dream recall sometimes get stuck early on thinking that they have forgotten the dream because they can't remember the entire thing. Start the practice early of honoring whatever it is you remember, even if it was only the small flash of a feeling or a single image. Short dreams or snippets are to be savored.

Quick Jot (Three Nouns)

)

)

)

Full Dream Date:

RECORD

Title:

Quick Jot (Three Nouns)

○

○

○

Full Dream Date:

Title:

Quick Jot (Three Nouns)

○

○

○

Full Dream Date:

RECORD

Title:

Quick Jot (Three Nouns)

○

○

○

Full Dream Date:

Title:

Quick Jot (Three Nouns)

○

○

○

Full Dream Date:

RECORD

Title:

Quick Jot (Three Nouns)

○

○

○

Full Dream Date:

Title:

Quick Jot (Three Nouns)

)

)

)

Full Dream Date:

RECORD

Title:

Quick Jot (Three Nouns)

- ○
- ○
- ○

Full Dream Date:

Title:

Quick Jot (Three Nouns)

)

)

)

_____

Full Dream Date:

Title:

Quick Jot (Three Nouns)

○

○

○

Full Dream Date:

Title:

Quick Jot (Three Nouns)

◯

◯

◯

Full Dream Date:

Title:

Quick Jot (Three Nouns)

○

○

○

Full Dream Date:

Title:

———— (((●))) ————

Quick Jot (Three Nouns)

)

)

)

Full Dream Date:

RECORD

Title:

———— (((●))) ————

Quick Jot (Three Nouns)

- ○
- ○
- ○

Full Dream Date:

Title:

Quick Jot (Three Nouns)

)

)

)

Full Dream Date:

RECORD

Title:

Quick Jot (Three Nouns)

- ○
- ○
- ○

Full Dream Date:

Title:

(((●))) ——

Quick Jot (Three Nouns)

)

)

)

Full Dream Date:

RECORD

Title:

(((●)))

Quick Jot (Three Nouns)

○

○

○

Full Dream Date:

Title:

Quick Jot (Three Nouns)

)

)

)

Full Dream Date:

RECORD

Title:

Quick Jot (Three Nouns)

○

○

○

Full Dream Date:

Title:

Quick Jot (Three Nouns)

)

)

)

Full Dream Date:

RECORD

Title:

Quick Jot (Three Nouns)

○

○

○

Full Dream Date:

Title:

Quick Jot (Three Nouns)

◯

◯

◯

Full Dream Date:

RECORD

Title:

Quick Jot (Three Nouns)

-
-
-

Full Dream Date:

Title:

Quick Jot (Three Nouns)

)

)

)

Full Dream Date:

Title:

Quick Jot (Three Nouns)

○

○

○

Full Dream Date:

Title:

Quick Jot (Three Nouns)

)

)

)

Full Dream Date:

RECORD

Title:

Quick Jot (Three Nouns)

○

○

○

Full Dream Date:

Title:

Quick Jot (Three Nouns)

)

)

)

Full Dream Date:

RECORD

Title:

Quick Jot (Three Nouns)

○

○

○

Full Dream Date:

Title:

Quick Jot (Three Nouns)

)

)

)

Full Dream Date:

Title:

Quick Jot (Three Nouns)

○

○

○

Full Dream Date:

Title:

Quick Jot (Three Nouns)

)

)

)

Full Dream Date:

RECORD

Title:

Quick Jot (Three Nouns)

○

○

○

Full Dream Date:

Title:

Quick Jot (Three Nouns)

○

○

○

Full Dream Date:

Title:

Quick Jot (Three Nouns)

○

○

○

Full Dream Date:

Title:

Quick Jot (Three Nouns)

)

)

)

Full Dream Date:

RECORD

Title:

Quick Jot (Three Nouns)

○

○

○

Full Dream Date:

Title:

Quick Jot (Three Nouns)

)

)

)

Full Dream Date:

RECORD

Title:

Quick Jot (Three Nouns)

○

○

○

Full Dream Date:

Title:

Quick Jot (Three Nouns)

○

○

○

Full Dream Date:

RECORD

Title:

Quick Jot (Three Nouns)

○

○

○

Full Dream Date:

Title:

Quick Jot (Three Nouns)

)

)

)

Full Dream Date:

RECORD

Title:

Quick Jot (Three Nouns)

○

○

○

Full Dream Date:

Title:

────── (((●))) ──────

Quick Jot (Three Nouns)

)

)

)

Full Dream Date:

RECORD

Title:

────── (((●))) ──────

Quick Jot (Three Nouns)

○

○

○

Full Dream Date:

Title:

Quick Jot (Three Nouns)

)

)

)

Full Dream Date:

Title:

Quick Jot (Three Nouns)

○

○

○

Full Dream Date:

Title:

Quick Jot (Three Nouns)

)

)

)

Full Dream Date:

Title:

Quick Jot (Three Nouns)

○

○

○

Full Dream Date:

Title:

((((●)))) ──────

Quick Jot (Three Nouns)

)

)

)

Full Dream Date:

RECORD

Title:

((((●)))) ──────

Quick Jot (Three Nouns)

○

○

○

Full Dream Date:

Title:

Quick Jot (Three Nouns)

○

○

○

Full Dream Date:

RECORD

Title:

Quick Jot (Three Nouns)

○

○

○

Full Dream Date:

Title:

Quick Jot (Three Nouns)

○

○

○

Full Dream Date:

Title:

Quick Jot (Three Nouns)

○

○

○

Full Dream Date:

Title:

(((●)))

Quick Jot (Three Nouns)

)

)

)

Full Dream Date:

Title:

(((●)))

Quick Jot (Three Nouns)

- ○
- ○
- ○

Full Dream Date:

Title:

Quick Jot (Three Nouns)

)

)

)

Full Dream Date:

RECORD

Title:

Quick Jot (Three Nouns)

○

○

○

Full Dream Date:

Title:

Quick Jot (Three Nouns)

)

)

)

Full Dream Date:

RECORD

Title:

Quick Jot (Three Nouns)

○

○

○

Full Dream Date:

Title:

Quick Jot (Three Nouns)

)

)

)

Full Dream Date:

RECORD

Title:

Quick Jot (Three Nouns)

○

○

○

Full Dream Date:

Title:

Quick Jot (Three Nouns)

)

)

)

Full Dream Date:

RECORD

Title:

Quick Jot (Three Nouns)

○

○

○

Full Dream Date:

Title:

Quick Jot (Three Nouns)

)

)

)

Full Dream Date:

RECORD

Title:

Quick Jot (Three Nouns)

○

○

○

Full Dream Date:

Title:

Quick Jot (Three Nouns)

)

)

)

Full Dream Date:

RECORD

Title:

Quick Jot (Three Nouns)

○

○

○

Full Dream Date:

Title:

Quick Jot (Three Nouns)

)

)

)

Full Dream Date:

Title:

Quick Jot (Three Nouns)

○

○

○

Full Dream Date:

Title:

Quick Jot (Three Nouns)

Full Dream Date:

RECORD

Title:

Quick Jot (Three Nouns)

○

○

○

Full Dream Date:

Title:

Quick Jot (Three Nouns)

○

○

○

Full Dream Date:

Title:

Want more information about how you can develop a transformative dream practice and get more out of this book?

Visit KeziaVida.com/thedreamingi. There you'll find a free introductory video about how to use this journal, a free mini course about How to Remember Dreams, and information about The Dreaming I Workshop a 28-day journey with this journal to cultivate a powerful relationship with your dreams.

Scan the code above to learn more!

DAILY DREAM PAGES

EXPLORE Daily dream pages are a method of dream exploration that works well with any dream. The central idea of the page is to separate the visual, auditory, or other information observed in the dream from the thoughts, feelings, and experiences that the dream invoked in you. This technique makes it easier to pick out the most potent elements of the dream. Outline the events in your dream from an objective perspective on the right (who, what, where, when, how), and a subjective perspective on the left (feelings, intuition, bodily sensations). Remember to check-in with your heart.

OBSERVATIONS

what did you see ○ hear ○ location
other people ○ actions taken

FEELINGS

how did you feel ○ why were you there ○
messages received

SCENE: Dark Theater watching a play.

Observer Awed by what person accomplished.

SCENE: Tattoo Factory where people were getting "spa"-like treatments plus tattoos. Like a factory conveyor belt. Grotesque people I was a participant
4/17/20

Scary feeling. Seductiveness of tattoos.

SCENE:

SCENE:

SCENE:

SCENE:

EXPLORE

OBSERVATIONS

FEELINGS

What was the deepest feeling in the dream? Can you locate it in your body? What's it like to try and feel it now? Easy, difficult? What comes up?

Is this feeling familiar? If so, identify specific examples. Or is this feeling new? If so, what does it remind you of?

COMMON DREAM FEELINGS ⊗

Fear	○ Joy	○ Connection	○ Need to Escape
Anxiety	○ Numbness	○ Desire	○ Distracted
Stress	○ Isolation	○ At Home	○ Confused
Tension	○ Power	○ Intimacy	○ Nurtured
Frustration	○ Anger	○ Peace	○ Passionate
Jealousy	○ Grief	○ Responsibility	○ Excited
Embarrassment	○ Pain	○ Frozen	○ Disgusted
Overwhelmed	○ Angst	○ Giddiness	○ Energized
Shame	○ Love	○ Awe	○ Guilt

○ { A } Light headed / Cloudy

○ { B } Jaw Clenched

○ { C } Throat Tight

○ { D } Shoulder Tension

○ { E } Chest Tight

○ { F } Pit in Stomach

○ { G } Aroused

○ { H } Weak Knees

○ { I } Weighed Down

EXPLORE

OBSERVATIONS

what did you see ⋄ hear ⋄ location
other people ⋄ actions taken

FEELINGS

how did you feel ⋄ why were you there ⋄
messages received

SCENE:

SCENE:

SCENE:

SCENE:

SCENE:

SCENE:

EXPLORE

OBSERVATIONS | **FEELINGS**

What was the deepest feeling in the dream? Can you locate it in your body? What's it like to try and feel it now? Easy, difficult? What comes up?

Is this feeling familiar? If so, identify specific examples. Or is this feeling new? If so, what does it remind you of?

⊗ COMMON DREAM FEELINGS ⊗

◯ Fear	◯ Joy	◯ Connection	◯ Need to Escape
◯ Anxiety	◯ Numbness	◯ Desire	◯ Distracted
◯ Stress	◯ Isolation	◯ At Home	◯ Confused
◯ Tension	◯ Power	◯ Intimacy	◯ Nurtured
◯ Frustration	◯ Anger	◯ Peace	◯ Passionate
◯ Jealousy	◯ Grief	◯ Responsibility	◯ Excited
◯ Embarrassment	◯ Pain	◯ Frozen	◯ Disgusted
◯ Overwhelmed	◯ Angst	◯ Giddiness	◯ Energized
◯ Shame	◯ Love	◯ Awe	◯ Guilt

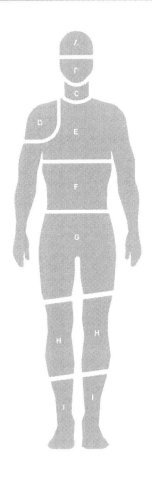

◯ { A } **Light headed / Cloudy**

◯ { B } **Jaw Clenched**

◯ { C } **Throat Tight**

◯ { D } **Shoulder Tension**

◯ { E } **Chest Tight**

◯ { F } **Pit in Stomach**

◯ { G } **Aroused**

◯ { H } **Weak Knees**

◯ { I } **Weighed Down**

EXPLORE

OBSERVATIONS

what did you see ◦ hear ◦ location
other people ◦ actions taken

FEELINGS

how did you feel ◦ why were you there ◦
messages received

SCENE:

SCENE:

SCENE:

SCENE:

SCENE:

SCENE:

EXPLORE

OBSERVATIONS   **FEELINGS**

What was the deepest feeling in the dream? Can you locate it in your body? What's it like to try and feel it now? Easy, difficult? What comes up?

Is this feeling familiar? If so, identify specific examples. Or is this feeling new? If so, what does it remind you of?

⊗ COMMON DREAM FEELINGS ⊗

⟩ Fear	○ Joy	○ Connection	○ Need to Escape
⟩ Anxiety	○ Numbness	○ Desire	○ Distracted
⟩ Stress	○ Isolation	○ At Home	○ Confused
⟩ Tension	○ Power	○ Intimacy	○ Nurtured
⟩ Frustration	○ Anger	○ Peace	○ Passionate
⟩ Jealousy	○ Grief	○ Responsibility	○ Excited
⟩ Embarrassment	○ Pain	○ Frozen	○ Disgusted
⟩ Overwhelmed	○ Angst	○ Giddiness	○ Energized
⟩ Shame	○ Love	○ Awe	○ Guilt

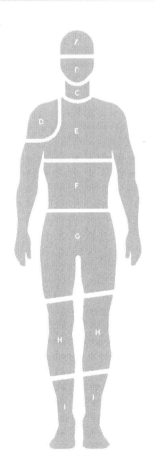

○ { A } Light headed / Cloudy

○ { B } Jaw Clenched

○ { C } Throat Tight

○ { D } Shoulder Tension

○ { E } Chest Tight

○ { F } Pit in Stomach

○ { G } Aroused

○ { H } Weak Knees

○ { I } Weighed Down

EXPLORE

OBSERVATIONS

what did you see ◦ hear ◦ location
other people ◦ actions taken

FEELINGS

how did you feel ◦ why were you there ◦
messages received

SCENE:

SCENE:

SCENE:

SCENE:

SCENE:

SCENE:

EXPLORE

OBSERVATIONS   **FEELINGS**

What was the deepest feeling in the dream? Can you locate it in your body? What's it like to try and feel it now? Easy, difficult? What comes up?

Is this feeling familiar? If so, identify specific examples. Or is this feeling new? If so, what does it remind you of?

⊗ COMMON DREAM FEELINGS ⊗

Fear	○ Joy	○ Connection	○ Need to Escape
Anxiety	○ Numbness	○ Desire	○ Distracted
Stress	○ Isolation	○ At Home	○ Confused
Tension	○ Power	○ Intimacy	○ Nurtured
Frustration	○ Anger	○ Peace	○ Passionate
Jealousy	○ Grief	○ Responsibility	○ Excited
Embarrassment	○ Pain	○ Frozen	○ Disgusted
Overwhelmed	○ Angst	○ Giddiness	○ Energized
Shame	○ Love	○ Awe	○ Guilt

○ { A } Light headed / Cloudy

○ { B } Jaw Clenched

○ { C } Throat Tight

○ { D } Shoulder Tension

○ { E } Chest Tight

○ { F } Pit in Stomach

○ { G } Aroused

○ { H } Weak Knees

○ { I } Weighed Down

OBSERVATIONS

what did you see ◦ hear ◦ location
other people ◦ actions taken

FEELINGS

how did you feel ◦ why were you there ◦
messages received

SCENE:

SCENE:

SCENE:

SCENE:

SCENE:

SCENE:

EXPLORE

OBSERVATIONS

FEELINGS

What was the deepest feeling in the dream? Can you locate it in your body? What's it like to try and feel it now? Easy, difficult? What comes up?

Is this feeling familiar? If so, identify specific examples. Or is this feeling new? If so, what does it remind you of?

COMMON DREAM FEELINGS

) Fear	○ Joy	○ Connection	○ Need to Escape
) Anxiety	○ Numbness	○ Desire	○ Distracted
) Stress	○ Isolation	○ At Home	○ Confused
) Tension	○ Power	○ Intimacy	○ Nurtured
) Frustration	○ Anger	○ Peace	○ Passionate
) Jealousy	○ Grief	○ Responsibility	○ Excited
) Embarrassment	○ Pain	○ Frozen	○ Disgusted
) Overwhelmed	○ Angst	○ Giddiness	○ Energized
) Shame	○ Love	○ Awe	○ Guilt

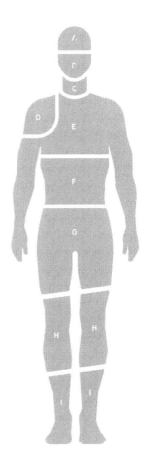

○ { A } Light headed / Cloudy

○ { B } Jaw Clenched

○ { C } Throat Tight

○ { D } Shoulder Tension

○ { E } Chest Tight

○ { F } Pit in Stomach

○ { G } Aroused

○ { H } Weak Knees

○ { I } Weighed Down

EXPLORE

115

OBSERVATIONS

what did you see ○ hear ○ location
other people ○ actions taken

FEELINGS

how did you feel ○ why were you there ○
messages received

SCENE:

SCENE:

SCENE:

CENE:

CENE:

CENE:

OBSERVATIONS

FEELINGS

EXPLORE

What was the deepest feeling in the dream? Can you locate it in your body? What's it like to try and feel it now? Easy, difficult? What comes up?

Is this feeling familiar? If so, identify specific examples. Or is this feeling new? If so, what does it remind you of?

△▽△▽△▽△▽△▽△▽△▽△▽△▽△▽△▽

⊗ COMMON DREAM FEELINGS ⊗

○ Fear
○ Anxiety
○ Stress
○ Tension
○ Frustration
○ Jealousy
○ Embarrassment
○ Overwhelmed
○ Shame

○ Joy
○ Numbness
○ Isolation
○ Power
○ Anger
○ Grief
○ Pain
○ Angst
○ Love

○ Connection
○ Desire
○ At Home
○ Intimacy
○ Peace
○ Responsibility
○ Frozen
○ Giddiness
○ Awe

○ Need to Escape
○ Distracted
○ Confused
○ Nurtured
○ Passionate
○ Excited
○ Disgusted
○ Energized
○ Guilt

○ { A } Light headed / Cloudy

○ { B } Jaw Clenched

○ { C } Throat Tight

○ { D } Shoulder Tension

○ { E } Chest Tight

○ { F } Pit in Stomach

○ { G } Aroused

○ { H } Weak Knees

○ { I } Weighed Down

EXPLORE

OBSERVATIONS

what did you see ◦ hear ◦ location
other people ◦ actions taken

FEELINGS

how did you feel ◦ why were you there ◦
messages received

SCENE:

SCENE:

SCENE:

SCENE:

SCENE:

SCENE:

EXPLORE

OBSERVATIONS

FEELINGS

What was the deepest feeling in the dream? Can you locate it in your body? What's it like to try and feel it now? Easy, difficult? What comes up?

Is this feeling familiar? If so, identify specific examples. Or is this feeling new? If so, what does it remind you of?

⊗ COMMON DREAM FEELINGS ⊗

- Fear
- Anxiety
- Stress
- Tension
- Frustration
- Jealousy
- Embarrassment
- Overwhelmed
- Shame

- Joy
- Numbness
- Isolation
- Power
- Anger
- Grief
- Pain
- Angst
- Love

- Connection
- Desire
- At Home
- Intimacy
- Peace
- Responsibility
- Frozen
- Giddiness
- Awe

- Need to Escape
- Distracted
- Confused
- Nurtured
- Passionate
- Excited
- Disgusted
- Energized
- Guilt

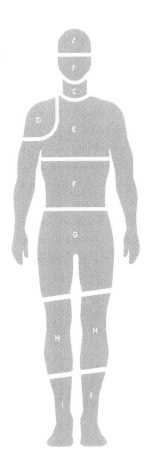

○ { A } Light headed / Cloudy

○ { B } Jaw Clenched

○ { C } Throat Tight

○ { D } Shoulder Tension

○ { E } Chest Tight

○ { F } Pit in Stomach

○ { G } Aroused

○ { H } Weak Knees

○ { I } Weighed Down

EXPLORE

OBSERVATIONS	FEELINGS
what did you see ◦ hear ◦ location other people ◦ actions taken	how did you feel ◦ why were you there ◦ messages received

SCENE:

SCENE:

SCENE:

SCENE:

SCENE:

SCENE:

EXPLORE

OBSERVATIONS   **FEELINGS**

What was the deepest feeling in the dream? Can you locate it in your body? What's it like to try and feel it now? Easy, difficult? What comes up?

Is this feeling familiar? If so, identify specific examples. Or is this feeling new? If so, what does it remind you of?

COMMON DREAM FEELINGS

Fear	○ Joy	○ Connection	○ Need to Escape
Anxiety	○ Numbness	○ Desire	○ Distracted
Stress	○ Isolation	○ At Home	○ Confused
Tension	○ Power	○ Intimacy	○ Nurtured
Frustration	○ Anger	○ Peace	○ Passionate
Jealousy	○ Grief	○ Responsibility	○ Excited
Embarrassment	○ Pain	○ Frozen	○ Disgusted
Overwhelmed	○ Angst	○ Giddiness	○ Energized
Shame	○ Love	○ Awe	○ Guilt

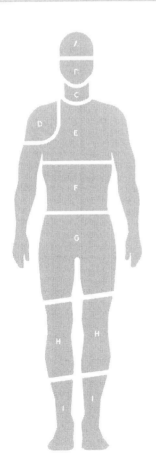

○ { A } Light headed / Cloudy

○ { B } Jaw Clenched

○ { C } Throat Tight

○ { D } Shoulder Tension

○ { E } Chest Tight

○ { F } Pit in Stomach

○ { G } Aroused

○ { H } Weak Knees

○ { I } Weighed Down

EXPLORE

OBSERVATIONS

what did you see ◦ hear ◦ location
other people ◦ actions taken

FEELINGS

how did you feel ◦ why were you there ◦
messages received

SCENE:

SCENE:

SCENE:

CENE:

CENE:

ENE:

EXPLORE

OBSERVATIONS | **FEELINGS**

129

What was the deepest feeling in the dream? Can you locate it in your body? What's it like to try and feel it now? Easy, difficult? What comes up?

Is this feeling familiar? If so, identify specific examples. Or is this feeling new? If so, what does it remind you of?

⊗ COMMON DREAM FEELINGS ⊗

○ Fear	○ Joy	○ Connection	○ Need to Escape
○ Anxiety	○ Numbness	○ Desire	○ Distracted
○ Stress	○ Isolation	○ At Home	○ Confused
○ Tension	○ Power	○ Intimacy	○ Nurtured
○ Frustration	○ Anger	○ Peace	○ Passionate
○ Jealousy	○ Grief	○ Responsibility	○ Excited
○ Embarrassment	○ Pain	○ Frozen	○ Disgusted
○ Overwhelmed	○ Angst	○ Giddiness	○ Energized
○ Shame	○ Love	○ Awe	○ Guilt

○ { A } Light headed / Cloudy

○ { B } Jaw Clenched

○ { C } Throat Tight

○ { D } Shoulder Tension

○ { E } Chest Tight

○ { F } Pit in Stomach

○ { G } Aroused

○ { H } Weak Knees

○ { I } Weighed Down

OBSERVATIONS

what did you see ◦ hear ◦ location
other people ◦ actions taken

FEELINGS

how did you feel ◦ why were you there ◦
messages received

SCENE:

SCENE:

SCENE:

SCENE:

SCENE:

SCENE:

EXPLORE

OBSERVATIONS

FEELINGS

133

What was the deepest feeling in the dream? Can you locate it in your body? What's it like to try and feel it now? Easy, difficult? What comes up?

Is this feeling familiar? If so, identify specific examples. Or is this feeling new? If so, what does it remind you of?

△▽△▽△▽△▽△▽△▽△▽△▽△▽△▽△▽

⊗ COMMON DREAM FEELINGS ⊗

Fear	○ Joy	○ Connection	○ Need to Escape
Anxiety	○ Numbness	○ Desire	○ Distracted
Stress	○ Isolation	○ At Home	○ Confused
Tension	○ Power	○ Intimacy	○ Nurtured
Frustration	○ Anger	○ Peace	○ Passionate
Jealousy	○ Grief	○ Responsibility	○ Excited
Embarrassment	○ Pain	○ Frozen	○ Disgusted
Overwhelmed	○ Angst	○ Giddiness	○ Energized
Shame	○ Love	○ Awe	○ Guilt

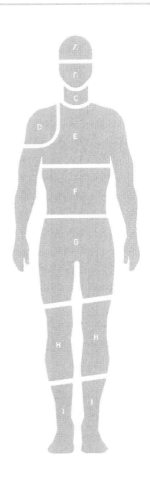

○ { A } Light headed / Cloudy

○ { B } Jaw Clenched

○ { C } Throat Tight

○ { D } Shoulder Tension

○ { E } Chest Tight

○ { F } Pit in Stomach

○ { G } Aroused

○ { H } Weak Knees

○ { I } Weighed Down

OBSERVATIONS

what did you see ◦ hear ◦ location
other people ◦ actions taken

FEELINGS

how did you feel ◦ why were you there ◦
messages received

SCENE:

SCENE:

SCENE:

SCENE:

SCENE:

SCENE:

EXPLORE

OBSERVATIONS

FEELINGS

What was the deepest feeling in the dream? Can you locate it in your body? What's it like to try and feel it now? Easy, difficult? What comes up?

Is this feeling familiar? If so, identify specific examples. Or is this feeling new? If so, what does it remind you of?

▲▼△▼△▼△▼△▼△▼△▼△▼△▼△▼△▼△▼△▼

⊗ COMMON DREAM FEELINGS ⊗

Fear	○ Joy	○ Connection	○ Need to Escape
Anxiety	○ Numbness	○ Desire	○ Distracted
Stress	○ Isolation	○ At Home	○ Confused
Tension	○ Power	○ Intimacy	○ Nurtured
Frustration	○ Anger	○ Peace	○ Passionate
Jealousy	○ Grief	○ Responsibility	○ Excited
Embarrassment	○ Pain	○ Frozen	○ Disgusted
Overwhelmed	○ Angst	○ Giddiness	○ Energized
Shame	○ Love	○ Awe	○ Guilt

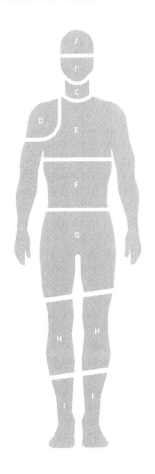

○ { A } Light headed / Cloudy

○ { B } Jaw Clenched

○ { C } Throat Tight

○ { D } Shoulder Tension

○ { E } Chest Tight

○ { F } Pit in Stomach

○ { G } Aroused

○ { H } Weak Knees

○ { I } Weighed Down

OBSERVATIONS

what did you see ◦ hear ◦ location
other people ◦ actions taken

FEELINGS

how did you feel ◦ why were you there ◦
messages received

SCENE:

SCENE:

SCENE:

CENE:

CENE:

ENE:

EXPLORE

OBSERVATIONS

FEELINGS

What was the deepest feeling in the dream? Can you locate it in your body? What's it like to try and feel it now? Easy, difficult? What comes up?

Is this feeling familiar? If so, identify specific examples. Or is this feeling new? If so, what does it remind you of?

⊗ COMMON DREAM FEELINGS ⊗

Fear	○ Joy	○ Connection	○ Need to Escape
Anxiety	○ Numbness	○ Desire	○ Distracted
Stress	○ Isolation	○ At Home	○ Confused
Tension	○ Power	○ Intimacy	○ Nurtured
Frustration	○ Anger	○ Peace	○ Passionate
Jealousy	○ Grief	○ Responsibility	○ Excited
Embarrassment	○ Pain	○ Frozen	○ Disgusted
Overwhelmed	○ Angst	○ Giddiness	○ Energized
Shame	○ Love	○ Awe	○ Guilt

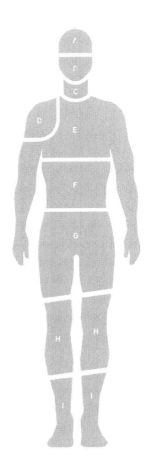

○ { A } Light headed / Cloudy

○ { B } Jaw Clenched

○ { C } Throat Tight

○ { D } Shoulder Tension

○ { E } Chest Tight

○ { F } Pit in Stomach

○ { G } Aroused

○ { H } Weak Knees

○ { I } Weighed Down

OBSERVATIONS

what did you see ◦ hear ◦ location
other people ◦ actions taken

FEELINGS

how did you feel ◦ why were you there ◦
messages received

SCENE:

SCENE:

SCENE:

SCENE:

SCENE:

SCENE:

EXPLORE

OBSERVATIONS

FEELINGS

What was the deepest feeling in the dream? Can you locate it in your body? What's it like to try and feel it now? Easy, difficult? What comes up?

Is this feeling familiar? If so, identify specific examples. Or is this feeling new? If so, what does it remind you of?

⊗ COMMON DREAM FEELINGS ⊗

Fear	○ Joy	○ Connection	○ Need to Escape
Anxiety	○ Numbness	○ Desire	○ Distracted
Stress	○ Isolation	○ At Home	○ Confused
Tension	○ Power	○ Intimacy	○ Nurtured
Frustration	○ Anger	○ Peace	○ Passionate
Jealousy	○ Grief	○ Responsibility	○ Excited
Embarrassment	○ Pain	○ Frozen	○ Disgusted
Overwhelmed	○ Angst	○ Giddiness	○ Energized
Shame	○ Love	○ Awe	○ Guilt

○ { A } Light headed / Cloudy

○ { B } Jaw Clenched

○ { C } Throat Tight

○ { D } Shoulder Tension

○ { E } Chest Tight

○ { F } Pit in Stomach

○ { G } Aroused

○ { H } Weak Knees

○ { I } Weighed Down

OBSERVATIONS

what did you see ○ hear ○ location
other people ○ actions taken

FEELINGS

how did you feel ○ why were you there ○
messages received

SCENE:

SCENE:

SCENE:

EXPLORE

CENE:

CENE:

ENE:

OBSERVATIONS

FEELINGS

What was the deepest feeling in the dream? Can you locate it in your body? What's it like to try and feel it now? Easy, difficult? What comes up?

Is this feeling familiar? If so, identify specific examples. Or is this feeling new? If so, what does it remind you of?

COMMON DREAM FEELINGS

Fear
Anxiety
Stress
Tension
Frustration
Jealousy
Embarrassment
Overwhelmed
Shame

○ Joy
○ Numbness
○ Isolation
○ Power
○ Anger
○ Grief
○ Pain
○ Angst
○ Love

○ Connection
○ Desire
○ At Home
○ Intimacy
○ Peace
○ Responsibility
○ Frozen
○ Giddiness
○ Awe

○ Need to Escape
○ Distracted
○ Confused
○ Nurtured
○ Passionate
○ Excited
○ Disgusted
○ Energized
○ Guilt

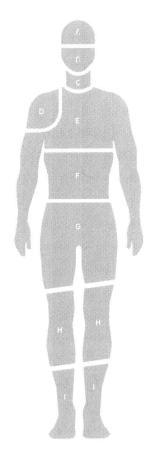

○ { A } Light headed / Cloudy

○ { B } Jaw Clenched

○ { C } Throat Tight

○ { D } Shoulder Tension

○ { E } Chest Tight

○ { F } Pit in Stomach

○ { G } Aroused

○ { H } Weak Knees

○ { I } Weighed Down

151

OBSERVATIONS

what did you see ◦ hear ◦ location
other people ◦ actions taken

FEELINGS

how did you feel ◦ why were you there ◦
messages received

SCENE:

SCENE:

SCENE:

CENE:

CENE:

ENE:

EXPLORE

OBSERVATIONS　　　**FEELINGS**

153

What was the deepest feeling in the dream? Can you locate it in your body? What's it like to try and feel it now? Easy, difficult? What comes up?

Is this feeling familiar? If so, identify specific examples. Or is this feeling new? If so, what does it remind you of?

▲▽▲▽▲▽▲▽▲▽▲▽▲▽▲▽▲▽▲▽▲▽▲▽▲▽

⊗ COMMON DREAM FEELINGS ⊗

Fear	○ Joy	○ Connection	○ Need to Escape
Anxiety	○ Numbness	○ Desire	○ Distracted
Stress	○ Isolation	○ At Home	○ Confused
Tension	○ Power	○ Intimacy	○ Nurtured
Frustration	○ Anger	○ Peace	○ Passionate
Jealousy	○ Grief	○ Responsibility	○ Excited
Embarrassment	○ Pain	○ Frozen	○ Disgusted
Overwhelmed	○ Angst	○ Giddiness	○ Energized
Shame	○ Love	○ Awe	○ Guilt

○ { A } **Light headed / Cloudy**

○ { B } **Jaw Clenched**

○ { C } **Throat Tight**

○ { D } **Shoulder Tension**

○ { E } **Chest Tight**

○ { F } **Pit in Stomach**

○ { G } **Aroused**

○ { H } **Weak Knees**

○ { I } **Weighed Down**

OBSERVATIONS

what did you see ◦ hear ◦ location
other people ◦ actions taken

FEELINGS

how did you feel ◦ why were you there ◦
messages received

SCENE:

SCENE:

SCENE:

SCENE:

SCENE:

SCENE:

EXPLORE

OBSERVATIONS   **FEELINGS**

What was the deepest feeling in the dream? Can you locate it in your body? What's it like to try and feel it now? Easy, difficult? What comes up?

Is this feeling familiar? If so, identify specific examples. Or is this feeling new? If so, what does it remind you of?

⊗ COMMON DREAM FEELINGS ⊗

Fear	○ Joy	○ Connection	○ Need to Escape
Anxiety	○ Numbness	○ Desire	○ Distracted
Stress	○ Isolation	○ At Home	○ Confused
Tension	○ Power	○ Intimacy	○ Nurtured
Frustration	○ Anger	○ Peace	○ Passionate
Jealousy	○ Grief	○ Responsibility	○ Excited
Embarrassment	○ Pain	○ Frozen	○ Disgusted
Overwhelmed	○ Angst	○ Giddiness	○ Energized
Shame	○ Love	○ Awe	○ Guilt

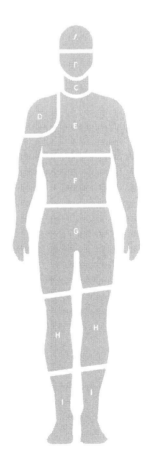

○ { A } **Light headed / Cloudy**

○ { B } **Jaw Clenched**

○ { C } **Throat Tight**

○ { D } **Shoulder Tension**

○ { E } **Chest Tight**

○ { F } **Pit in Stomach**

○ { G } **Aroused**

○ { H } **Weak Knees**

○ { I } **Weighed Down**

OBSERVATIONS | ## FEELINGS

what did you see ◦ hear ◦ location
other people ◦ actions taken

how did you feel ◦ why were you there ◦
messages received

SCENE:

SCENE:

SCENE:

CENE:

CENE:

ENE:

EXPLORE

OBSERVATIONS　　　　　　FEELINGS

161

What was the deepest feeling in the dream? Can you locate it in your body? What's it like to try and feel it now? Easy, difficult? What comes up?

Is this feeling familiar? If so, identify specific examples. Or is this feeling new? If so, what does it remind you of?

△▽△▽△▽△▽△▽△▽△▽△▽△▽△▽△▽△▽

⊗ COMMON DREAM FEELINGS ⊗

Fear	○ Joy	○ Connection	○ Need to Escape
Anxiety	○ Numbness	○ Desire	○ Distracted
Stress	○ Isolation	○ At Home	○ Confused
Tension	○ Power	○ Intimacy	○ Nurtured
Frustration	○ Anger	○ Peace	○ Passionate
Jealousy	○ Grief	○ Responsibility	○ Excited
Embarrassment	○ Pain	○ Frozen	○ Disgusted
Overwhelmed	○ Angst	○ Giddiness	○ Energized
Shame	○ Love	○ Awe	○ Guilt

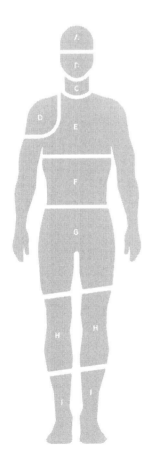

○ { A } Light headed / Cloudy

○ { B } Jaw Clenched

○ { C } Throat Tight

○ { D } Shoulder Tension

○ { E } Chest Tight

○ { F } Pit in Stomach

○ { G } Aroused

○ { H } Weak Knees

○ { I } Weighed Down

EXPLORE

OBSERVATIONS

what did you see ◦ hear ◦ location
other people ◦ actions taken

FEELINGS

how did you feel ◦ why were you there ◦
messages received

SCENE:

SCENE:

SCENE:

CENE:

CENE:

ENE:

EXPLORE

OBSERVATIONS

FEELINGS

What was the deepest feeling in the dream? Can you locate it in your body? What's it like to try and feel it now? Easy, difficult? What comes up?

Is this feeling familiar? If so, identify specific examples. Or is this feeling new? If so, what does it remind you of?

▲▽△▽△▽△▽△▽△▽△▽△▽△▽△▽

⊗ COMMON DREAM FEELINGS ⊗

○ Fear	○ Joy	○ Connection	○ Need to Escape
○ Anxiety	○ Numbness	○ Desire	○ Distracted
○ Stress	○ Isolation	○ At Home	○ Confused
○ Tension	○ Power	○ Intimacy	○ Nurtured
○ Frustration	○ Anger	○ Peace	○ Passionate
○ Jealousy	○ Grief	○ Responsibility	○ Excited
○ Embarrassment	○ Pain	○ Frozen	○ Disgusted
○ Overwhelmed	○ Angst	○ Giddiness	○ Energized
○ Shame	○ Love	○ Awe	○ Guilt

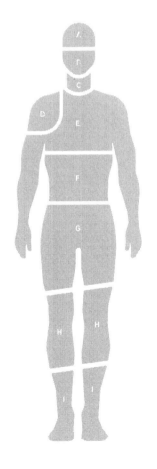

○ { A } Light headed / Cloudy

○ { B } Jaw Clenched

○ { C } Throat Tight

○ { D } Shoulder Tension

○ { E } Chest Tight

○ { F } Pit in Stomach

○ { G } Aroused

○ { H } Weak Knees

○ { I } Weighed Down

OBSERVATIONS

what did you see ◦ hear ◦ location
other people ◦ actions taken

FEELINGS

how did you feel ◦ why were you there ◦
messages received

SCENE:

SCENE:

SCENE:

CENE:

CENE:

ENE:

EXPLORE

OBSERVATIONS   **FEELINGS**

What was the deepest feeling in the dream? Can you locate it in your body? What's it like to try and feel it now? Easy, difficult? What comes up?

Is this feeling familiar? If so, identify specific examples. Or is this feeling new? If so, what does it remind you of?

COMMON DREAM FEELINGS ⊗

○ Fear	○ Joy	○ Connection	○ Need to Escape
○ Anxiety	○ Numbness	○ Desire	○ Distracted
Stress	○ Isolation	○ At Home	○ Confused
○ Tension	○ Power	○ Intimacy	○ Nurtured
Frustration	○ Anger	○ Peace	○ Passionate
Jealousy	○ Grief	○ Responsibility	○ Excited
Embarrassment	○ Pain	○ Frozen	○ Disgusted
Overwhelmed	○ Angst	○ Giddiness	○ Energized
Shame	○ Love	○ Awe	○ Guilt

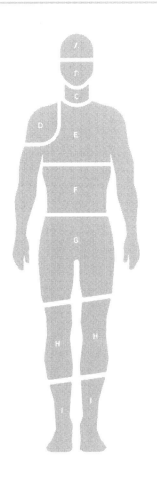

○ { A } Light headed / Cloudy

○ { B } Jaw Clenched

○ { C } Throat Tight

○ { D } Shoulder Tension

○ { E } Chest Tight

○ { F } Pit in Stomach

○ { G } Aroused

○ { H } Weak Knees

○ { I } Weighed Down

EXPLORE

171

OBSERVATIONS

what did you see ○ hear ○ location

other people ○ actions taken

FEELINGS

how did you feel ○ why were you there ○

messages received

SCENE:

SCENE:

SCENE:

SCENE:

SCENE:

SCENE:

OBSERVATIONS **FEELINGS**

What was the deepest feeling in the dream? Can you locate it in your body? What's it like to try and feel it now? Easy, difficult? What comes up?

Is this feeling familiar? If so, identify specific examples. Or is this feeling new? If so, what does it remind you of?

⊗ COMMON DREAM FEELINGS ⊗

Fear	○ Joy	○ Connection	○ Need to Escape
Anxiety	○ Numbness	○ Desire	○ Distracted
Stress	○ Isolation	○ At Home	○ Confused
Tension	○ Power	○ Intimacy	○ Nurtured
Frustration	○ Anger	○ Peace	○ Passionate
Jealousy	○ Grief	○ Responsibility	○ Excited
Embarrassment	○ Pain	○ Frozen	○ Disgusted
Overwhelmed	○ Angst	○ Giddiness	○ Energized
Shame	○ Love	○ Awe	○ Guilt

○ { A } **Light headed / Cloudy**

○ { B } **Jaw Clenched**

○ { C } **Throat Tight**

○ { D } **Shoulder Tension**

○ { E } **Chest Tight**

○ { F } **Pit in Stomach**

○ { G } **Aroused**

○ { H } **Weak Knees**

○ { I } **Weighed Down**

EXPLORE

OBSERVATIONS

what did you see ○ hear ○ location
other people ○ actions taken

FEELINGS

how did you feel ○ why were you there ○
messages received

SCENE:

SCENE:

SCENE:

SCENE:

SCENE:

SCENE:

EXPLORE

OBSERVATIONS　　　**FEELINGS**

What was the deepest feeling in the dream? Can you locate it in your body? What's it like to try and feel it now? Easy, difficult? What comes up?

Is this feeling familiar? If so, identify specific examples. Or is this feeling new? If so, what does it remind you of?

⊗ COMMON DREAM FEELINGS ⊗

Fear	○ Joy	○ Connection	○ Need to Escape
Anxiety	○ Numbness	○ Desire	○ Distracted
Stress	○ Isolation	○ At Home	○ Confused
Tension	○ Power	○ Intimacy	○ Nurtured
Frustration	○ Anger	○ Peace	○ Passionate
Jealousy	○ Grief	○ Responsibility	○ Excited
Embarrassment	○ Pain	○ Frozen	○ Disgusted
Overwhelmed	○ Angst	○ Giddiness	○ Energized
Shame	○ Love	○ Awe	○ Guilt

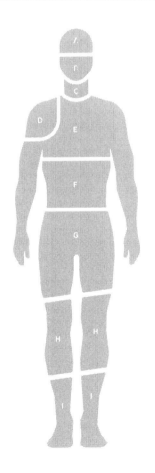

○ { A } **Light headed / Cloudy**

○ { B } **Jaw Clenched**

○ { C } **Throat Tight**

○ { D } **Shoulder Tension**

○ { E } **Chest Tight**

○ { F } **Pit in Stomach**

○ { G } **Aroused**

○ { H } **Weak Knees**

○ { I } **Weighed Down**

EXPLORE

REFLECTION In the following pages, you'll find ten different ways that you can dive even more deeply into your dream practice. The last two exercises are designed to help you create a personal dream glossary, collecting dream images and moments that you experience along your dream journey with this book in a way that supports you and your dreaming. The rest of the exercises were created to be used with a particular dream.

TYPE OF DREAM	DREAM EXERCISE
dreams that seem obvious mundane / boring dreams	connecting dreams to waking life — Pg. 190
dreams with intense emotions / visceral dreams	feeling your dreams — Pg. 196
dreams you can't remember well	create a dream map — Pg. 200
detailed dreams / dreams with twists and turns	identifying triggers in dreams — Pg. 204
dreams with hard, painful emotions and/or nightmares	the power of hard dreams — Pg. 208
weird dreams / strange dreams / paranormal dreams	all dreams are weird — Pg. 212
dreams that aren't for you / dreams about TV or movies	your dreams are yours — Pg. 216
unforgettable dreams / remarkable dreams	dreams as inspiration — Pg. 222
repetitive dreams / reoccurring dreams	write your own dream dictionary — Pg. 226
any dream that makes you feel good	your dreams love you — Pg. 236

EXPLORING YOUR DREAM LIFE

Answer these questions when you have space and time. If an answer doesn't come easily, feel free to take a pause and come back to the question later. Stretch your imagination and arouse your intuition.

◉ **What do you daydream about most often?**

What professional achievement would be a 'dream come true'?

What is your pipe dream?

⊙ **What family, community, state, U.S. and/or global issues keep you up at night?**

⊙ **Do you have any repetitive or reoccurring dream themes / characters?**

What are your current sleeping habits? How many hours per night do you sleep on average? What are you bedtime / morning rituals or patterns?

Have you ever felt disturbed, distressed, or upset by your dreams? When and why?

◉ **What dream do you remember most vividly in your life?**

◉ **What's the most beautiful thing you ever saw in a dream?**

What would your dream relationship / partnership be like (romantic or otherwise)?

What does a dream life look like to you?

REFLECT

◉ **What does your body dream of?**

◉ **What does your mind dream of?**

What does your soul dream of?

CONNECTING DREAMS TO WAKING LIFE

Sometimes, we awaken from dreams that feel very familiar to us. The dream can directly reference a situation at work or in our relationships, or simply reflects a familiar feeling or dynamic from waking life. You might assume the dream has no meaning, or that the dream is merely pointing out what you already know. Use the exercise below for dreams like this.

FOR: DREAMS WITH OBVIOUS MEANINGS, BORING DREAMS, MUNDANE DREAMS

Begin by releasing all of your ideas/judgments in regards to what this dream is about. Open to the dream by assuming that your waking mind does not know what this dream means. Walk through the dream slowly with your mind's eye and try to re-experience it as fully as possible.

After completing this, focus on the most familiar part of the dream. How long can you linger on this part of the dream before getting distracted? Spend some time tapping in now. Keep returning until you can feel the feeling for 10 full seconds.

Now, spend the next week paying as much attention as you can to when that particular situation or experience arises in your daily life. Record it in the chart that follows. Be open to surprises as to when and where this familiar experience arises.

Date / Time	Setting (Before / After)	Duration	Intensity (1-5)

Date / Time	Setting (Before / After)	Duration	Intensity (1-5)

REFLECT

Date / Time	Setting (Before / After)	Duration	Intensity (1-5

Date / Time	Setting (Before / After)	Duration	Intensity (1-5)

REFLECT

FEELING YOUR DREAMS

One way to expand and deepen the power of your dream practice is to focus on experiencing your dreams and the feelings that arise from them with as much presence and respect as you can muster. This is a unique approach to dreamwork that privileges the felt experience of your dream over any kind of objective analysis or interpretation that the mind has to offer. Use this exercise to explore feelings in dreams.

FOR: DREAMS WITH INTENSE EMOTIONS OR FEELINGS

Identify the strongest feeling in your dream and connect with it inside of your body.

(((●)))

Imagine this feeling is an object. Using your intuition,
consider everything objective you can about this thing--i.e.,
its size, shape, color, location, etc. Use the power of your
imagination to give the feeling a form.

Once you have an object/form for your feeling,
imagine placing it in your hands, or bringing it closer
to you in some way. What feelings arise then? How
easy/hard is this to do?

REFLECT

Using your intuition, ask, if this feeling had a home
in your body, where would it live?

○ { A } Light headed / Cloudy

○ { B } Jaw Clenched

○ { C } Throat Tight

○ { D } Shoulder Tension

○ { E } Chest Tight

○ { F } Pit in Stomach

○ { G } Aroused

○ { H } Weak Knees

○ { I } Weighed Down

Draw a sketch / free write about the feeling and you in
the space below

CREATE A DREAM MAP

If you are simply looking for an out of the box way to explore the conter of your dreams, this is one of my favorite methods. It can help you spark your imagination and creativity if you feel like a dream is unclear or stucl

FOR: **ANY DREAM, DREAMS YOU CAN'T REMEMBER WELL**

To create a dream map, brainstorm all of the things you saw in your dream: locations, people, objects, words, feelings, sensations. Then choose the most compelling part of the dream and place it in the center. You can write a few words, draw a symbol, or draw a sketch to represent this part of the dream.

Then, consider the next part of the dream that comes to mind, and draw/write/symbolize it somewhere else on the paper, connecting it to the first thing you drew with a line or arrow. (If you're feeling boxed in by the space provided, feel free to draw your own!)

Continue this process until your entire dream has been mapped out. You can always feel free to draw multiple connection lines to various aspects of the dream, as well as map out content that may not have been present in the dream but hold relevance to the dream (i.e. memories, associations, etc…).

REFLECT

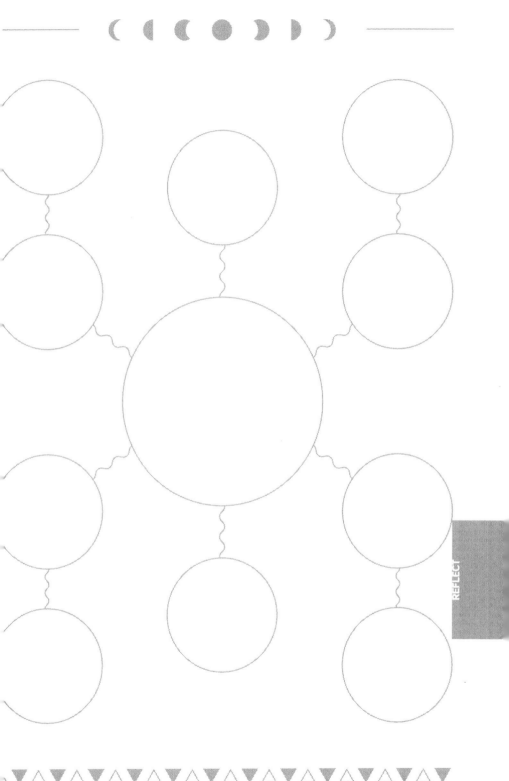

REFLECT

IDENTIFYING TRIGGERS IN DREAMS

When it comes to actualizing our dreams and ambitions, one of the biggest obstacles we face is releasing past traumas and learning to cope when we are triggered. Dreams can be an excellent ally in this process. Use the exercise below to learn how to utilize your dream material in this way.

FOR: HIGHLY DETAILED DREAMS, DREAMS THAT SHIFT SUDDENLY

Outline the events of the dream on
the time line to the right.

REFLECT

Looking at the time line, use your intuition to identify a turning point in the dream and record it below. Was there a moment in the dream after which everything changed? Keep in mind that there may be more than one turning point in the dream.

If you could accept for a moment that this feeling/experience is related to a difficult situation from your past, what would it be? Use your intuition here, whatever arises is worthwhile information.

REFLECT

Review the rest of the feelings/events in the dream that happened after the turning point. How are they connected to each other? How are they similar/different than the feelings that arose the past situation you identified above?

THE POWER OF HARD DREAMS

As you deepen your dream practice, you may encounter difficult things in your dreams. To work these dreams, it helps to believe your dreams want to support you. Trusting this fully is a long path--the first step is accepting it is a possibility. Here's an exercise to help you recognize the support available in dreams.

FOR: DREAMS WITH HARD, PAINFUL EMOTIONS, NIGHTMARES, NIGHT TERRORS

Recall your dream in your mind's eye, taking an outsider's view on the scene. Become a witness to yourself in the dream. How many nouns (persons, places, or things) can you identify? Take note of each them on the following page.

REFLECT

Date:

○   ○

○   ○

○   ○

○   ○

○   ○

Date:

○   ○

○   ○

○   ○

○   ○

○   ○

Date:

○   ○

○   ○

○   ○

○   ○

○   ○

With each thing that you have identified, see it alone in your minds eye. Is it possible to imagine that this thing as supportive in any way? Go through each person, place, or thing listed with that question in mind. If 's possible to feel it's supportive, receive the sensation of support that is available for you. Use blank paper to sketch, free write, or identify words that reflect the feeling of support.

To Go Deeper...

If you discover that there is something supportive in the dream, attempt to feel the difficult feeling in the dream at the same time you feel the sense of support...or as close to the same time as you can. Play with this, bringing the feelings of support and the painful/scary emotion together.

If nothing in the dream that you observed could feel supportive, consider if there are any dreams you have ever had where you felt loved and supported. Go back to one of those moments in dreams, and bathe yourself in that feeling of support, and then do the work above.

If you can't recall ever feeling supported or loved in a dream, you can also use a memory from waking life, grounding yourself in a sense of being supported before becoming vulnerable to the intensity of emotion found in the dream.

REFLECT

ALL DREAMS ARE WEIRD

Dream experience can be understood to serve as a balance to our waking experience on emotional, mental, and spiritual levels. To recognize these lessons, become a detective in your dreams. Precisely witness discrepancies between the dream and your waking life. These differences can be obvious or subtle. Where you find them, there is often wisdom about how to balance your perspective, your actions, and your feelings.

FOR: **WEIRD DREAMS, PARANORMAL DREAMS, FANTASTICAL DREAMS**

Compare and contrast your dream
and your waking life.

SAME | DIFFERENT

SAME

DIFFERENT

What do you find most strange about the dream?
How could this bring balance to some aspect of your life?

What do you find most unimportant in your dream?
How could this bring balance to some aspect of your life?

YOUR DREAMS ARE YOURS

Sometimes, the content of dreams can lead us to conclude that our dream wasn't for us. Maybe our dream was caused by watching a TV show or our dream has a message for someone else. These things could certainly be true, but we honor the depth of our dreams by taking a both/and perspective and considering also that our dreams are ours. When we take full ownership of our dreams, we allow them to show us the path back to wholeness.

FOR: DREAMS ABOUT TV/MOVIES, DREAMS THAT AREN'T ABOUT YOU

Record your dream at right from the POV of someone or something else in the dream. If there's someone in the dream you think the dream is for, take their perspective. If there are no characters or objects in the dream, feel free to write from the 3rd person perspective.

Record Below

List at least 5 images or words that symbolize or reflect the way the dream feels from this alternative perspective.

Now, write the dream from your own POV.

List at least 10 images or words that symbolize or reflect
the way the dream feels from your perspective.

○ ○   ○   ○   ○   ○   ○   ○   ○   ○   ○   ○   ○   ○   ○   ○   ○

Review your lists and choose the 3 that feel the most
distant/ you have the most trouble feeling connected to.

○ ○ ○ ○ ○ ○ ○ ○ ○ ○ ○ ○ ○ ○ ○ ○

Choose the most distant feeling of the three and
do the following meditation.

Bring this feeling into your heart. Release your judgment, associations, or ideas about the source of this feeling. Just for the next five minutes, accept that this feeling is an aspect of your being. Each time resistance to this idea arises, observe th nature of the resistance. Visualize the resistance separating from you and take one more step towards the feeling itself. Practice this meditation with any feeling in a dream that feels like it is not for you.

REFLECT

DREAMS AS INSPIRATION

Dreams have an amazing capacity to spark our imagination and our curiosity. When a dream captures your attention and you can't seem to forget it, trust that it has a depth for you to uncover over time. Use the dream as a jumping off board for any creative project that you are working on or when you need new insight on a problem you've been wrestling with. Below is a list of ways that you can use to spark your creativity or cultivate inspiration.

FOR: DREAMS YOU CAN'T FORGET

Make a collage of your favorite dream moments and insights. Grab som glue sticks, scissors, markers/colored pencils, watercolors---whatever yc feel most comfortable being creative with and try to fill the page with a of the images from the dream.

Take a person or even an object from one of your dreams and write a poem or monologue about the dream from their/its perspective. Or, just write the dream you had, from the perspective of someone else in the dream.

Write down at least five different ways you could understand the significance of your dream. Bonus if some of those ways conflict directly with each other.

Make a comic strip out of your dream--draw in stick figures. Challenge yourself to stay true to the order of the events as you remember them even if they seem irrational.

Create a soundtrack to your dream--which songs go perfectly with which parts? Or does it inspire a whole list of songs? Make a play list of your dream on your favorite music app to listen to whenever you want!

REFLECT

Act the dream out in your living room. Go through the motions and the gestures that you remember feeling in the dream, and embody the emotional content. Say whatever words come to you to say out loud. If you're really brave, invite sacred witnesses to your performance.

Act the dream out in your living room. Go through the motions and the gestures that you remember feeling in the dream, and embody the emotional content. Say whatever words come to you to say out loud. If you're really brave, invite sacred witnesses to your performance.

Create an abstract drawing or painting from your dream. Make no effort to create something aesthetically pleasing. Instead, focus your attention on the experience of your dream and imagine that your pen or brush is expressing it to paper.

Write down your dream. Then take all the words that you have just written down and rearrange them into a poem.

Connect a dream to a movie or TV show that you know well. Recast the characters or even objects in your dream as famous actors. What genre would your dream be in? How big of a budget would it need to be produced? Where would you film your dream?

Take a dream that ends abruptly and continue the narrative. What happens next? What do you say, do, see or feel? Keep going until the dream feels complete.

Create an altar to your cherished dream. Fill it with objects and images that remind you of the dream experience. Use the altar to set intentions and express gratitude to the dream time.

Turn your dream into a prayer.

Do something in real life that you did in a dream. Choose something practical and physically safe--i.e. Visiting an accessible location from a dream, reaching out to an old friend that appeared in a dream, eating a certain food present in a dream.

Post your dream in an on line group or on social media and ask people for their feedback and impressions (set any boundaries you'd like in terms of what you'd like comments on or not).

When an animal or other element of nature appears in your dream, take the time to research how that element functions and arises in nature and reflect on how those functions and abilities could be useful to you.

REFLECT

Make up your own creative process with your dream! Share it with the hashtag #thedreamingi :)

WRITE YOUR OWN DREAM DICTIONARY

Use the space below to make note of recurring scenes, people, objects, or situations in your dreams over time. When you notice repetitive people, places, or situations in your dreams, there's a good chance there's a powerful lesson available for you. Consider each time they appear an opportunity to learn more about your personal symbolism.

◎ ◎ ◎ ◎ ◎ ◎ ◎ ◎ ◎ ◎

FOR: WHEN YOU AWAKE THINKING--I'VE HAD THIS DREAM BEFORE!

◎ ◎ ◎ ◎ ◎ ◎ ◎ ◎ ◎ ◎

Dream Motif: Person, place, feeling, thing.

Associations: What do you associate w/ this motif, i.e. your attitudes, memories, feelings, etc? Answer for here and now.

Symbolism: What could this person/place/thing symbolize for you personally, right here and now? Stretch yourself to think of something new each time.

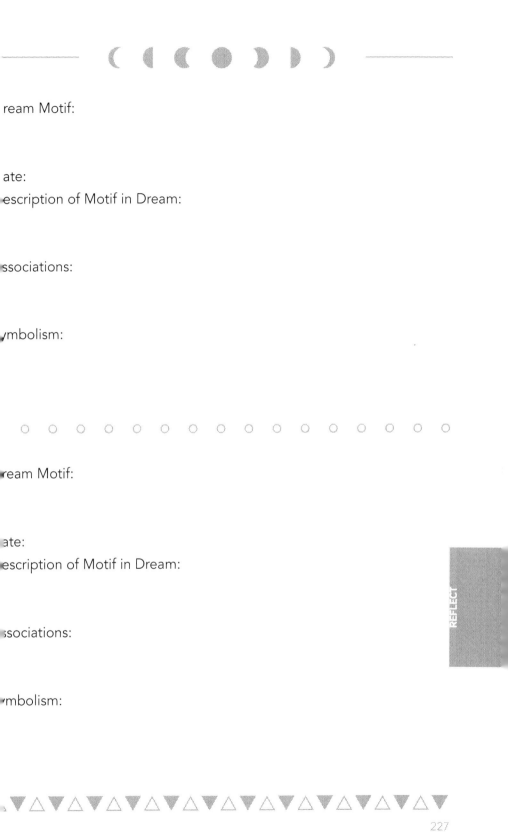

ream Motif:

ate:

escription of Motif in Dream:

ssociations:

mbolism:

ream Motif:

ate:

escription of Motif in Dream:

ssociations:

mbolism:

Dream Motif:

Date:
Description of Motif in Dream:

Associations:

Symbolism:

Dream Motif:

Date:
Description of Motif in Dream:

Associations:

Symbolism:

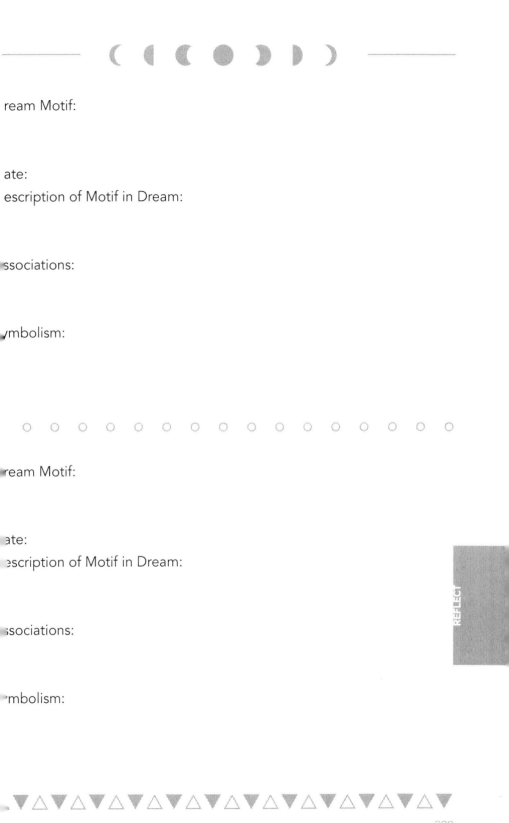

ream Motif:

ate:
escription of Motif in Dream:

ssociations:

ymbolism:

○ ○ ○ ○ ○ ○ ○ ○ ○ ○ ○ ○ ○ ○ ○ ○

ream Motif:

ate:
escription of Motif in Dream:

ssociations:

mbolism:

REFLECT

Dream Motif:

Date:
Description of Motif in Dream:

Associations:

Symbolism:

Dream Motif:

Date:
Description of Motif in Dream:

Associations:

Symbolism:

ream Motif:

ate:
escription of Motif in Dream:

ssociations:

ymbolism:

ream Motif:

ate:
escription of Motif in Dream:

ssociations:

mbolism:

REFLECT

Dream Motif:

Date:
Description of Motif in Dream:

Associations:

Symbolism:

Dream Motif:

Date:
Description of Motif in Dream:

Associations:

Symbolism:

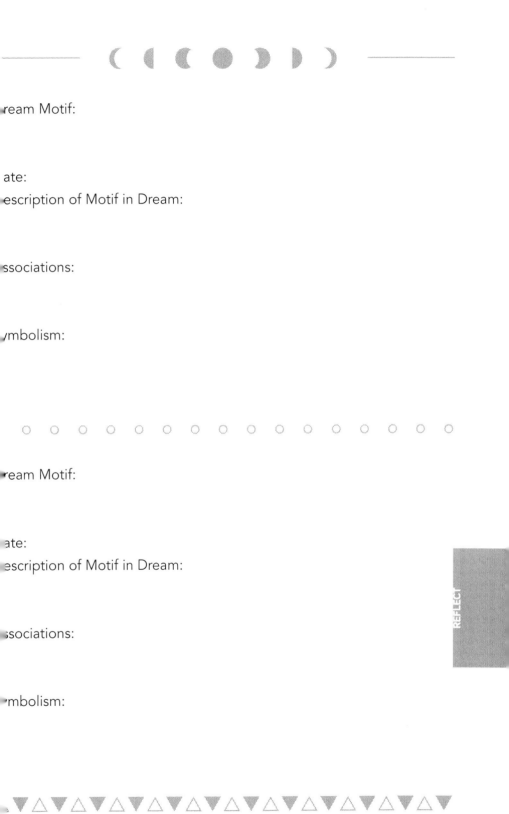

Dream Motif:

Date:
Description of Motif in Dream:

Associations:

Symbolism:

Dream Motif:

Date:
Description of Motif in Dream:

Associations:

Symbolism:

Dream Motif:

Date:
Description of Motif in Dream:

Associations:

Symbolism:

○ ○ ○ ○ ○ ○ ○ ○ ○ ○ ○ ○ ○ ○ ○

Dream Motif:

Date:
Description of Motif in Dream:

Associations:

Symbolism:

ream Motif:

ate:
escription of Motif in Dream:

ssociations:

ymbolism:

eam Motif:

ate:
escription of Motif in Dream:

ssociations:

mbolism:

YOUR DREAMS LOVE YOU

One of the most powerful things available to us in our dreams are incredible feelings support, inspiration, love, excitement, desire, passion wonder, gratitude, and awe that can arise in them. These dream experiences are truly divine gifts. It can be easy to overlook these moments in dreams--sometimes they come in small packages. Savor them. The more you allow them to take root in your consciousness, the stronger you will become.

FOR: DREAMS THAT MAKE YOU FEEL GOOD

In the pages that follow, sketch, write, or record any and every dream moment that has ever inspired you. Record anything in your dream that depicts gratitude, love, connection, hope, or awe. Capture the essence of the uplifting feeling in the dream here and refer to this gallery of support whenever you need a pick-me-up.

REFLECT

REFLECT

REFLECT

CONTINUING THE PRACTICE

Want more information about how you can develop a transformative dream practice and get more out of this book?

Visit KeziaVida.com/thedreamingi. There you'll find a free introductory video about how to use this journal, a free mini course about How to Remember Dreams, and information about The Dreaming I Workshop, a 28-day journey with this journal to cultivate a powerful relationship with your dreams.

Scan the code above to learn more!

Made in the USA
Middletown, DE
30 January 2020

83974986R00137